I love that you're my

Mother-In-Law

because

Copyright © 2018 River Breeze Press
All rights reserved. This book or any portion thereof
may not be reproduced or used in any manner whatsoever without the express written permission of the publisher.

I Love You Because Books
www.riverbreezepress.com

To My Mother-In-Law

Love, _____

Date: _____

The best thing about you is your

_____

Thank you for being patient with me when

_____

You are better than

_____

You should win the grand prize for

_____

You make me feel special when

_____

I think it's awesome that you can

_____

I love to hear about when you

_____

I love when we

_____

together

You taught me how to

_____

I know you love me because

_____

I wish I could

_____

as well as you do

I love that we have the same

_____

You should be the queen of

_____

If you were a plant you would be a

_____

You make me laugh when you

_____

I wish I had more time to

_____

with you

You make the best

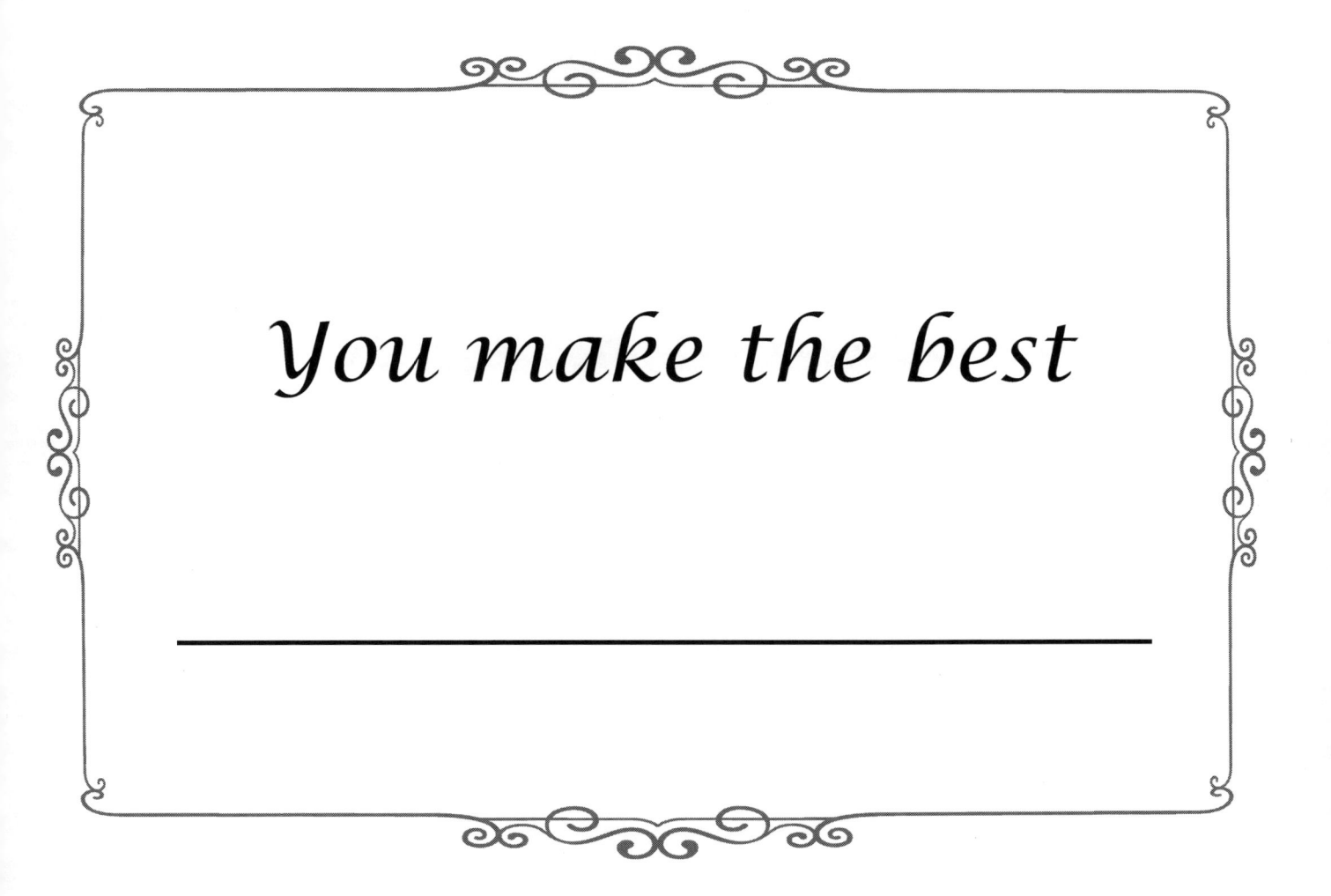

_____

You have inspired me to

_____

If I could give you anything it would be

_____

I would love to go

_____

with you

You are there for me when

_____

I love you because you are

_____

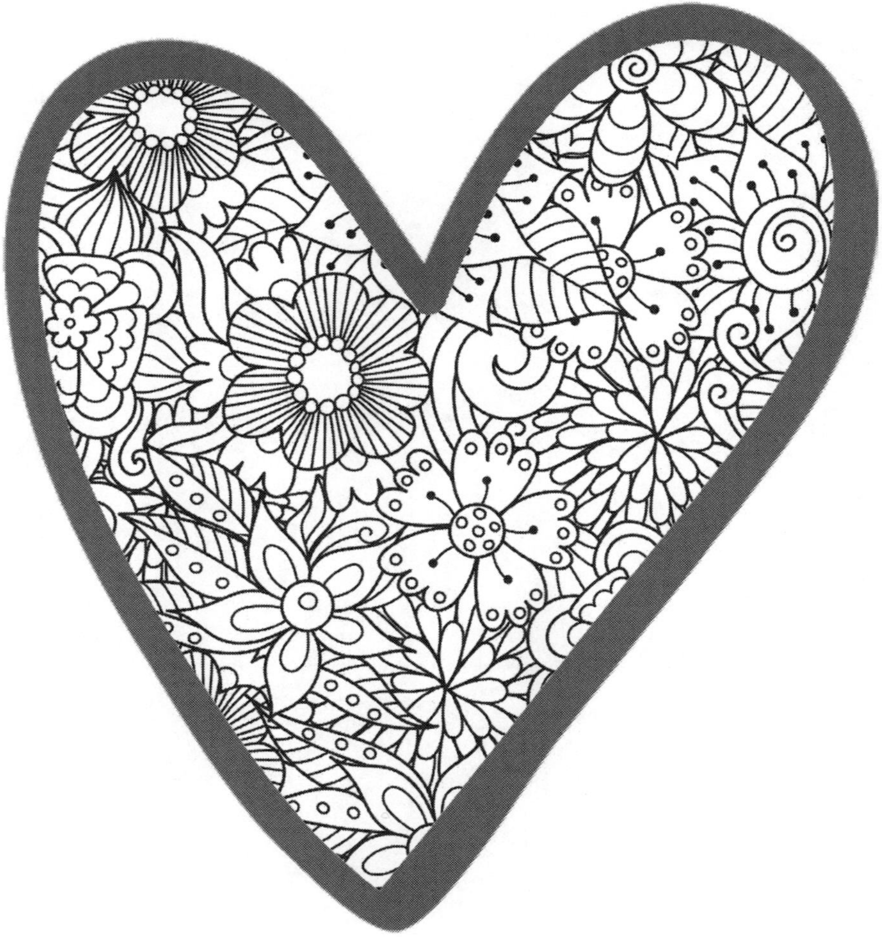

Made in the USA
Columbia, SC
30 December 2024